That's My Dog!

I HAVE A BOXER

By Benjamin Proudfit

Gareth Stevens
PUBLISHING

Please visit our website, www.garethstevens.com. For a free color catalog of all our high-quality books, call toll free 1-800-542-2595 or fax 1-877-542-2596.

Library of Congress Cataloging-in-Publication Data
Names: Proudfit, Benjamin, author.
Title: I have a boxer / Benjamin Proudfit.
Description: Buffalo : Gareth Stevens Publishing, 2026. | Series: That's my dog! | Includes index.
Identifiers: LCCN 2024034407 | ISBN 9781482469905 (library binding) | ISBN 9781482469899 (paperback) | ISBN 9781482469912 (ebook)
Subjects: LCSH: Boxer (Dog breed)–Juvenile literature.
Classification: LCC SF429.B75 P76 2026 | DDC 636.73–dc23/eng/20240905
LC record available at https://lccn.loc.gov/2024034407

First Edition

Published in 2026 by
Gareth Stevens Publishing
2544 Clinton Street
Buffalo, NY 14224

Editor: Kristen Nelson
Designer: Leslie Taylor

Photo credits: Cover, p. 1 ibanezfilm/Shutterstock.com; pp. 5, 11, 23 Pixel-Shot/Shutterstock.com; p. 7 BCFC/Shutterstock.com; pp. 9, 24 (coat) nik174/Shutterstock.com; p. 11 TamaraLSanchez/Shutterstock.com; pp. 13, 24 (ears) BIGANDT.COM/Shutterstock.com; p. 15 Benjamin Lyberg/Shutterstock.com; p. 17 Elena11/Shutterstock.com; p. 19 CeltyCrow/Shutterstock.com; pp. 21, 24 (cuddle) olgaarmawir/Shutterstock.com.

Printed in China

CPSIA compliance information: Batch #QS26GS: For further information contact Gareth Stevens, New York, New York at 1-800-542-2595.

Contents

This my dog.
His name is Titan.
He is a boxer.

Boxers have big heads.
They have droopy eyes.

They have short coats.
They feel smooth.

Titan has soft ears.
He likes it when I
pet them!

Boxers need to play a lot.
Titan and I run
in the yard together.

We take long walks.

Boxers are smart dogs. We took Titan to a training class.

I give Titan toys.
He likes to tug!

Boxers like to cuddle.
Titan lays with me.

Titan is the best dog.

I love my boxer!

Words to Know

coat

cuddle

ears

Index